POETICALLY BLESSED

POETICALLY BLESSED

Poetry

by

Maude "Candy" McDonald

POETICALLY BLESSED

by

Maude "Candy" McDonald

This book or parts thereof may not be reproduced in any form, by any means electronic, mechanical, photocopy, recording, or otherwise without prior written permission of the publisher, except as provided by United States of America copyright law.

        Copyright 2011 Maude "Candy" McDonald
                  All rights reserved
                      ISBN-13 9780615882604

DEDICATION

This book is dedicated to my late mother and father, Dorothy McDonald-Johnson and Harold McDonald who encouraged me to share my poetry at an early age, and to my son Jordan Walker for the continued push.
I love you "J"

ACKNOWLEDGEMENT

First, I give all the glory and honor to Jesus Christ, my lord and savior. I thank him for the gift of poetry and the gentle push to finally share it.

To my late parents Harold and Dorothy McDonald who encouraged and supported me in any endeavor I wanted to explore.

To my son Jordan walker who has definitely been a bright light in my life. My protector, bodyguard, and so much more. As we always say before we leave each other I love you, love you more, love you times infinity that's that stay focused and be Blessed.

To my brothers Gregory and David McDonald, my sister Renee McDonald, my sister in-law Stephanie. Thanks for being a part of my life and all that I have been through. Thanks for your support and putting up with me. I love you.

To my nieces, nephews, cousins, co-workers, associates, thank you for looking at my work and asking what are you waiting on? I appreciate your honesty.

Thanks to Wanda Shazell for the constant push.

Thank you Beverly Nelson for editing and critiquing my work.

Thanks to Leonard and Kimberly Falana you know why.

Special thanks to Timeco Ruth and Lisa Butler for being there and not letting any of my ways, tone of voice, my hard looks deter our friendship and for putting me in check when needed that's true unconditional friendship. "I got you dawg" smile

To my therapist Bernadette Ackerman thank for opening the tunnel so I could see the light.

Now for those of you who decided to take a chance on me I LOVE YOU! !

A God given gift, should be a gift shared
Expect and accept your blessings.
Enjoy.

mmcd

POETICALLY BLESSED

MY BLACK MAN

MY BLACK MAN satisfies me when the world
has tossed me around.
He sits me on a throne and my servant is he.
He's rough, but oh so gentle.
He soothes my body with just one touch.
This is why my black man means so much.

Knowing all he must go through,
This keeps me waiting honest, and true.

MY BLACK MAN satisfies me when the world
has brought me down.
It's like treating a child to the circus,
and he's the clown.
He touches my body, mind, and soul.
And after that, I'm no longer in control.

MY BLACK MAN satisfies me and this is why,
When I'm with him, there's no need to cry.

I LOVE MY BLACK MAN AND YOU WONDER WHY.

SISTER TO SISTER

I want you to know I can feel your pain

We're both the same just called by different names.

You will get through this I can promise you that.

Because, a few years ago I wore the same hat.

The journey gets a little bit easier with each passing day.

If you feel and believe it stop for a minute and pray.

Don't for once think you are in this alone and if you do just pick up the phone.

I know you can make it and you will get through

Sister to sister, me and you

WAS IT YOURS?

You took something that wasn't yours.
Shattered windows, broken doors, minds stripped of
Peace and security.
Something that once was beautiful is now ugly.

Was it yours?

You lied when you said you were my protector and
That there was no need to worry.
Now I blame myself for not keeping my guard up, but
You were not supposed to be the enemy.

The clock that once kept accurate time no longer
Ticks even when replaced with a new battery it
Refuses to work.

Was it yours?

The taking of ones mind, body and soul.
The backbone, the strong one no longer lives locked
In a shell with nothing left to give.

Was it yours?

MY ANGEL

God dispatched an angel who did all kinds of things
There's only one thing that's different this angel has
No wings.

She has a piercing knowledge that chizeled down one
Of the strongest walls, and during your weakest moments.

She gives strength to stand tall and helps you to see the things
You have accomplished, when you think you have done
nothing at all.

My angel is a sounding board, when I think there is no one to
Listen and lets me cry, when the world said I couldn't.

My angel is loving and caring.
I love my angel because god dispatched her especially for
me.
My angel

This is dedicated to Mrs. Bernadette Ackerman

THANK YOU

I want to say thank you
For all you have done for me
You removed the blinders from my eyes
When I couldn't see.

I have to say thank you for loving me
In spite of myself, when I thought there
Was no way out and put my life on a shelf

I want to say thank you for letting me
Knows I wasn't by myself.

I have to say thank you for blessing me
And surrounding me with a strong Family.

It's time to unite and forget the past.
Enjoy each other because time is
Moving to fast.

God made you and he made me, together
We are family.

For all you do
I say thank you

IT WAS MEANT TO BE

It was meant to be,
The union of you and me.
The hours we spent together
Was like uncovering lost treasure.
The times when we were separated
Was almost too much to bear;
But the separation made me see
Just how much I care.
They said it wouldn't last
And that was years ago,
We're still together
And much farther we will go.
It's obvious they had no knowledge
Of what they were talking about.
It's you and I together
Just like we started out.
If only they would see
Our love was meant to be.

THE ROSE, THE CHILD

So precious the Rose
Whose life is so short~

So cherish that Rose
Like your loved one's heart

So precious the child
Who's loved for a while
And then just left alone~

So precious the child
Who knows not a home
All he knows is to wander and roam.

So pamper the child as the rose
Love and nurture so he will grow
You must be careful for he is delicate too
Give him a chance to let his love come through.

STOP AND THINK

Stop and think
My brother, my lover, my friend
Do you want to be extinct?

You will if you don't stop and think

The game you're playing is so
Very wrong
Stop all the foolishness, stand up and be
Strong
Stop and think
You didn't make it this far because of
Who you are

Stop and think

We all need you here with us day to day.
We don't want to drive to a museum to
See a black man's face

Stop and think
If you keep playing into their hands
My brother, my lover, my friend
I just shutter to think my black man will
Be extinct

Please stop and think

BLACK

Way back black

Depressed and oppressed

Shackled and hung black.

Being pushed around

Raped and abused, black

No respect on the other side of the track, black

Denied and accused, black

Lied to and misused

Coming together, black

Sunday go to meeting and

Praising God, black

Equally black

Educated and in control, black

Moving forward, black

Showing the way, black

No longer in the back, black

Trying, striving, succeeding

You come a long way, black

If time should come and

I have to reconsider

No thanks,

I'd do it, all again, black

JUSTIFIED

Justified they cried

You don't know a thing about discrimination

Until you walked in our shoes

You can't sing my song

You don't know a damn thing about the blues

Justified you say because you see it your way

But if you see it through our eyes once again you

Would see you lied.

How can you say my feet don't hurt

You ain't walked in my tight ass shoes

Or traveled through hells dirt

Justified you say that only

Cause you see it your way

Justified

But not today!

POETICALLY BLESSED

Confused, frustrated, and often stressed I
Stop to ponder how did I get in this mess

Turn my head to the sky- deep within, but
Refusing to cry

Then words so melodically come my way I
Thank god and he says there's no need to
Stress along with everything else you're
Poetically blessed.

So like an electrical shock to the system I
Hold my head up and continue to listen.

He said I'm giving you something that's
Special to me so share it with others it will
Bring changes just wait and see.

The words I give to you will help others not
To stress you know why because you're
Poetically blessed.

So for now on the words that I send your
Way don't keep them to yourself you just
Might be able to keep someone from going
Astray.

So go on and don't stress you're my child
Along with being poetically blessed.

FOR YOU FOR ME

I'll be your flower if you'll be my sun to wake me in the morning when a new day has come.

I'll be your bucket if you'll be my rain. Well comfort each other through all sorrow and pain.

I'll be your seed if you'll be my soil protect me and give me the proper things for sufficient growth.

I'll be your moon if you'll be my stars. Holding on to what we have near or far.

I'll be your girl if you'll be my guy. Together we can make it if only we try. For you, For me

LONELINESS CAME

Loneliness came and conquered my soul, It's grip
was so tight I lost control.

Loneliness came a month after he left. It
slapped me in the face and in my bed It slept.

Loneliness woke me early in the morning and dragged
me through the day.

How will I make it with Loneliness leading the way?

Loneliness came and conquered my soul. I had a talk
with loneliness and now I'm in full control.

THAT TREE

I'm amazed at that tree

It stood there laughing

And waved at me.

Don't tell me I'm wrong

I know what I see

It started again

But now it's pointing at me.

Now that it's dark

I can barely see

That beautiful tree

Laughing at me.

SHE CLOSED HER EYES

She closed her eyes and went on home
Leaving me here all alone

She left me with a Hole in my Heart
No energy or desire to make a new
start

She left when she knew that our work
wasn't through
I wanted to carry on like mother and
daughter use to do

She left me here, and I don't know what
to do
We were mother and daughter, but
the best of friends too

Why did she leave - I guess I'll never
know,
All I do know is she's gone and I just
can't let go

LET IT GO

The past is gone
So let it go
The things you did then are now no more
The life you live depends on you
Forget yesterday, for today's brand new
There's no need to hold on, for it can't be changed
Let It Go

Set your goals, strive, and let nothing stand in your way
of what you want
The road to success is hard, but in the end it will mean more
to you
Stand up in your defense for what you believe
If it means you no good
Let It Go

In this lifetime and through it all, you have to walk, but you're
bound to fall
Don't hold it in Let It Out
As long as you live and wherever you go there are some things
in life you must LET GO

FROM THIS DAY ON

From this day on, I'm leaving you behind.
From this day on, I won't have you on my mind.
From this day on, I don't want my phone to ring.
From this day on, our favorite song I'll no longer sing.
From this day on, I guess you know we're through.
From this day on, there's no more me and you.
From this day on…

MEMORANDUM

TO: MY LOVE

FROM: YOURS

DATE: FOREVER

RE: MY LIFE

My life's complete when you are there, and I know it will last forever.

My life's complete when I am the one you share your joys as well as sorrows~

My life's complete when we have a disagreement, and we together come to terms and find what's wrong and not who's wrong.

My life's complete when we have conquered all obstacles that once stood in our way.

YES, MY LIFE'S COMPLETE WITH YOU

SEVEN SEAS

My Man gave me his hand and committed his life to me

Then he got in his boat and sailed the Seven Seas

He sailed the Seas for many years and I would often hear that He was doing just fine and would see me in a short time

A short time past and I never heard of Him or the Seven Seas

My Man gave me his hand, but His heart belonged to the Seven Seas

STANDSTILL

In this world I wonder
And often I ask why?
My life is at a standstill
As time goes flying by.
I know that I am missing
Whatever life holds;
I don't need priceless silver
Or even worthless gold,
I just want peace
To conquer my miserable soul.
The world just keeps turning
And my life is standing still,
I know I can make it
It's a must and I will.
I often ask why?
My soul continues to cry,
I know within my heart
And I just cannot lie.
In this world I wonder
And often ask why?
But that was yesterday
So I bid misery good-bye.

THROUGH THE EYES OF ANOTHER

I want to see myself through the eyes of another

Through the eyes of my Mother, what kind of daughter
have I been?
I would like to think I have done the right things
you have wished of me.
I know there have been times when
I was hard to reach, and you probably didn't know
what to do with me.
I'm glad you kept me and helped me to grow.
I just hope one day I can be as great
a Mother as you have been.

Through the eyes of my Brother,
what kind of sister have I been?
I know there have been times
when I acted just like a boy and wanted
to follow you around.
Who else could I turn to?
I didn't have a big sister to help me out.
Thanks, for the protection and the screening
of my dates. Thanks, I needed you
and you were there.

Through the eyes of my Lover, I do not have to ask
what kind of lover I was, I know.
You were my first love, and you taught me well.
Thank you for the natural high, and for one solid
year of my life, I stayed that way.
Thank you for the nights I spent alone
waiting for you to phone.
Thanks for the hell you put me through.
I had to love you to withstand those flames.
Thanks to you, I'm a lot tougher now;
and where I used to smile, I now wear a frown.

Through my eye, I don't know.
Now, I see myself.
I have a somewhat sorted view.
If you had walked the paths that I have,
maybe, you would too.

SECRETLY

Secretly I watch the way you walk and attentively
I listen when you talk.

Secretly I stare when you enter the room and hope
that you don't notice me watching you only.

Secretly my heart skips beats when you are near
but you'll never know it's my Secret Dear.

Secretly I wonder if you are watching me too and
just what you are thinking when you smile the way
you do.

Secretly I admire whatever I want to and see it
the way it pleases me. No one can stop me or
dare to interrupt.

No one can take what is secretly yours. You hold
the keys to the Secret doors.

Secretly

THANKS, BUT NO THANKS

You set me free,
but still I'm a slave to your inequality.
You took the shackles off my ankles and wrist
and put them on my brain restricting my education.
Thanks, but no thanks.

You called me names, and raped our mothers;
You beat our fathers and hung our brothers;
and still, I emerged.
Thanks, but no thanks.

Still today, you want to have it your way
With the things you say and do;
Wait a minute there
That was yesterday!
Thanks, but no thanks.

IN SPITE OF IT ALL

Life has tossed and turned you like some toy
ball and used you for whatever they could

You have got pure hell from Day one and continue
to catch hell In so many aspects of life

In spite of all, you still remain and hide the
pain that torments you over and over again

This is why I can look beyond you faults and
downfalls and say I Love You
In Spite of it All

HER STORY, HER SONG

Listen to the story the wind told.
She stepped right up and chilled my very soul.
She assured me that nothing was wrong but, yet she kept singing her song.

She told of stories from the past until now.
She kept on singing and then she sat down.
I stared with great amazement and through all the amazement I saw her crown.

Then I noticed as others gathered around.
She was oh so beautiful and her skin was so fair.
A moment passed and she vanished into thin air.
I will never forget her story, her song.

"LITTLE RED SCHOOL HOUSE"

The Little Red School House that granny told me bout,
You went and got your lesson and you dare not pout.
You didn't talk back like the children do today.
Cause you look at the floor and that's where you lay.
The Little Red School House that granny told me bout
Was filled with love and learning, and you were what
The teacher cared about.
The Little Red School House where it al I began
And all children walked hand in hand.

SOUL TO MIND

Soul said Mind
Where did you Go
Hither and Yonder
to and fro

Searching and Seeking
for things unknown
Trials and Tribulations
Through them I've grown

Soul said Mind
Where have you been
Seeking and Searching
For a Real and True friend

Soul said mine
Where have you Gone
Traveled to the past to see
what I've done
Where can I go to ease my mind
Troubles troubling all the time

BROKEN WING

The broken wing of a bird enables it
To soar
To leave the nest and explore the
Wonders of this world
The broken winged bird is a wounded
Creature, fearing all around him,
Trusting no one
Can't you see the hurt in his eye when
You try to assist in any way to ease
His pain and bring comfort
How can a bird fly with a broken
Wing, can one ever love with a broken
Heart
Time will heal the broken wing. What
Will time do for the hurting heart

MY HISTORY BOOK

My history book stands about 5 feet, 11 inches
and does not move too fast.
My history book has seen,
and even lived, the events.
Therefore, I can get it firsthand.

You don't have to read this book
because it talks to you.
Just sit down and ask the questions
that most often come to mind.
My Grandmother and Great Grandmother
are my history books.
They have seen and lived the events
that are so often misprinted,
or not printed at all.

She doesn't move too fast now, but once she did.
Because she had no other choice
with Master right behind her.
Why don't you spend some time with her
and find out just what did happen.
There's no charge for this lesson,
and you won't be mislead.

Their history books left a lot unsaid.
I turned to my Grandmother,
and got the truth instead.

SEARCHING

I went to the waters to free my soul

I went to the waters and that's where my troubles began to unfold

I went to the waters to sooth my mind
During the soothing, I lost track of time

I stared in the waters and myself, I did see
The longer I stared, the more of me I began to see

I went to the waters to free my soul

I left the old me there and the new me took control

DO THE RIGHT THING

You gave her a ring
So make her heart
The journey you are on is about to
End count it all joy, that's the
Past a new life is about to begin

Do the right thing
You gave her a ring so make
Her heart sing
You want to be the man that she
Needs and wants to be around
Forever.

Do the right thing
You gave her a ring so make her
Heart sing
A real woman stands by her man
Through thick and thin.
She was good enough to have your
Child go head man walk her down the
Aisle

Do the right thing make her heart
Sing

NO END

Disillusioned
Mass Confusion
Anger everywhere
Rape and Murder
Violence on the Rise
Drug Abuse
Insanity Running Loose

No End My Friend

He took his life
She took someone else's
Everybody taking something that's not theirs
to take in first place
Hatred and haste
Minds going to waste
Nothing is safe and sacred
No one cares but everyone dares
Lies and Spies
Sinking ships
Sending rockets off making Blank trips
No one's trusting, no one's trusted
Drug dealers and users
Minds have rushed
Our loves dying everyday
Even the children, they try
and snatch them away

No End My Friend

She likes my man
He likes her man
What a Jam
No one's discrete
Be Bold, Do It In The Street
Disillusioned
Mass Confusion

NO END

IT'S TIME TO PRAY

When the one you love has gone astray and
Worries grow day by day

It's time to pray

When the wells of the eye overflow with
Tears and fear becomes your constant
Companion

It's time to pray

When the walls seem tot closing in on you
And there is no exit door.

It's time to pray

When the burden is too heavy and you can't
Take no more

It's time to pray

When you don't know what to say just fall
On your knees, lift up your head,
Acknowledge him and he'll do the rest he's
Our father and he knows what's best

Pray

THIS DAY

This day be ours
From now until

This love everlasting
by the Master's will

This ring I give
Has no end
Compared to our planet
It has a continuous spin

My love to you
I freely give
From this day on
As one we will live

Remember the vows
We have just taken
Loving one another and
All others shall be forsaken

This day be ours
From now until

SIMPLE THINGS IN LIFE

Running Free
Finding Me
For I've gotten lost along the way

Taking time to smell the flowers
Slowly walking through the showers

Whatever happen to the simple things
in life that use to make one happy

The smiling face and the
innocent hello
The time when one was in love
they seem to glow

Everything is so rush, rush now
We have all forgotten
The simple things in life

STRANGE

Strange is the man
and strange is he
Stranger than anything
You would ever want to see

This man was strange
In the way he dressed
I asked him why
He said it was his best

Strange was the look upon his face~
He appeared to be quite confused
and new to this place

Strange was this man
and Strange indeed
I don't know, he could be saying
The same about me!

MY PROMISE

I make this promise to you my son
To guide and protect you until the day is done

To love and lead you in the best way I know how.
Teach you to pray and thank God everyday.

Encourage and caress you when the journey seems rough

Cuddle and kiss you until you say enough, hold and rock
You until you slumber deep

Then smile as I watch my beautiful child sleep.

This is my promise

FAMILY FIRST

Jesus said I'm watching you
And this is what I want you
To do

Keep the family first after me
Of course
This may be hard at times
But never give up
And always keep in mind
One doesn't make a family

Jesus said I'm watching and
This is what I expect you
To do
Raise the youth in my house
Show them the way I've
Shown you
Let them know how important
Family is and that one
Doesn't make a family

Keep the family first after me
Of course
Family First

TEARS OF HOPE

Tears so many tears
What makes you cry? Those lonely tears, is it the pan or hidden
Fears.

There's someone to talk to if you would just take time, let go
Of those troubles and comfort you will find

Tears so many tears
Don't give up, help is on the way. Stand still and in time we will
Find the strength to endure all that will come our way

There will be tears of hope, tears of joy, tears cried for
Every man, woman, girl and boy
Tears of hope

Tears I'm finding the comfort that I need to keep moving on and
Now I believe there are, tears of hope, tears of joy, tears for
Every man, woman, girl and boy

Understanding tears, never misleading
Tears of hope

ONE TREE … MANY BRANCHES

As you light each candle, in memory of us …
The ones who have hone home …
Don't weep, no fuss
For we all have journeyed on

No, don't say it or one time think you are alone …
For you have each other near or far …
You are one tree … but many branches …
Starting from the same root …

The light you see has glow …
It's there to let you know …
We are all fine; one tree … many branches

One tree many branches …
Now it's all up too you to keep it together
To raise the children the way we did you …

So when the time comes …
And our earthly candles do dim …
We won't have to worry because you know
What you have taught them …
One strong root … one tree many branches
And beautiful memories

DESTINY

Destiny where has thou taken me? To the
Highest of the highs and the lowest of
Lows.
You have taken me to love.
I stay, but love goes.

Destiny where has thou taken me?
To the bed sides of many who I have loved
And known, some are in heaven and me
Once again left alone

Destiny oh destiny
The journeys been long, but every now
And then there has been some happy
Songs

Destiny has guided me thru dark tunnels
To the light but~ when I needed a friend I
Ran into a dead end.

Destiny oh destiny
Where does this journey take me. ?
You planned it all so tell me, which way to go

Destiny oh destiny
Only you know my destiny

THE KEY TO MY HOUSE
IS THE KEY TO MY HEART

I gave you the key to my house,
That open the door, but the key
You hold opens so much more

The key to my house is the key
To my heart you opened the door
And began to create some beautiful art.

Then all of a sudden it began to
Come apart I didn't understand
This was not part of the plan

Yes I'm old school and you be hip hop
We said at the start this was no reason to stop

The key to my house was the key to my heart.
The key that you hold no longer lets you in either one.
You may be hip hop and I may be old school to set the record
Straight you aint dealing with no old fool.

MY LOVE FOR YOU

My love for you I cant explain.
A smile just automatically comes to my face when I call your name
I love to cuddle my little pooh. I thank god each day for giving me you
Its not easy being away I'm used to seeing you everyday
My day is so empty & my nights are so long. I wonder if you hear me when I
Sing our song.
Even though I'm away. I miss you sweetie in so many ways my love for you I
Wont explain

HOLD MY HAND

Mom and dad please understand I am
Starting out in a brand new and,
I don't know what's ahead
I'm your child, hold my hand

The people that surround me will
All be new. They won't be my old
Teachers and they won't be you.
Don't leave me stranded, hold my hand

All I'm asking of you is to remember
That I'm part of you. I'm not grown, I
Have a ways to go and a lot to learn
Hold my hand

They say when I'm little I'm on your
Lap and when I'm big I'm on your
Heart, but until 1 can half way
Figure out some of my future plans
Promise me you will hold my hand

Hold my hand

For the graduating Head Start Class 2011

HANG IN THERE

They say that the eyes are a
Mirror to the soul.
I feel your pain even though my
Ears, your story you haven't
Told.
I want you to know it will be
All right in due time, but you
Have to hang in there
Know that the master has your
Back.
When you feel all has let you
Down, let a smile replace that
Frown.

Hang in there

HAPPY MOTHERS DAY

I just want to sa y on your special da y that l love you in so many ways.

I know some times I make you mad, but still you love me.

I make a mess, but still you love me

I stay up pass my bed time and don't want to get up in the
Morning, but still you love me

There is no other like you mother
I love you

Happy Mothers Day

NO BITCH NO WHORE

No bitch no whore

You said it once don't say it no more

Do these words ever mess with your head when you are cuddling and
Caressing lying in bed?

No bitch no whore

You said it once don't say it no more

You have a mother, a sister, and an aunt and a lot of other ladies in your
Life using names like that do you really think it's right?

No bitch no whore

You have used it so loosely and for so very long you got us dancing to it
While you sing it in your songs.

I ain't no bitch

I ain't no whore

That's it

No more

THE N-WORD IN THREE

When you say the n-word it comes in three that's my brother, my
Sister and me. The n-word you may take for a joke but maybe you
Wouldn't if at that time in life you were me. It all started when we
Moved from the north to the south by the urging of my auntie.
That's when I was introduced to the n-word, but don't forget the n-
Word came in three that's my brother, my sister and me.

In Springfield Mass, we all lived together on a paved street and at the
End was a circle where we all would often meet. I didn't have to
Worry about heat or somewhere to go because where I came from
There was entertainment and there was snow.

We walked to school together as a group all races hand in hand, but
That was up north , but in the south we walked a dirt road and
Caught the bus that's not all we caught. We caught the n-word in
Three.

When we arrived at Idylwild Elementary in the year 65 I think it was
Only my brother, my sister and me believe it the n-word was served to
Us like it was a delicacy. That's one reason why I can't find a place for
It in my vocabulary.

So when I hear the n-word I don't hurt for me I hurt for three

My brother Gregory

My sister Renee

And me

The n-word you cease to be

ABOUT THE AUTHOR

Maude McDonald better known as "Candy" was born in Springfield, Mass. and raised in St. Petersburg, FL. Maude is a graduate of Florida State University with an Undergraduate Degree in Early Childhood Education. She has been writing since grade school. In 1999 and 2000 she has received awards for outstanding achievement and excellence in poetry. In 1993 she traveled to Washington, D.C. and was inducted into the International Society of Poets. In 1994 an article was placed in the Minuteman Airforce reserve magazine about the poetry she wrote during Desert Shield/Storm. Her work has appeared in various anthologies including the teachers anthology in 1989. She lives in St. Petersburg, Florida with her son Jordan and dog Eli.

Pictures by: Stevie Rogers
Hair by: Shawna Chance of Divine Textures
Makeup by: Heather Jackson at Dillard's at Tyrone Mall
Clothes selected by: Jordan Walker
Contact information: mcdonaldmaude@gmail.com
Maujor Productions

www.ingramcontent.com/pod-product-compliance
Lightning Source LLC
Chambersburg PA
CBHW081502040426
42446CB00016B/3354